English Olympiad

Book 8

© **B. Jain Publishers (P) Ltd.** All rights reserved. No part of this book may be reproduced, stored in a retrieval system or transmitted, in any form or by any means, mechanical, photocopying, recording or otherwise, without any prior written permission of the publisher.

Published by Kuldeep Jain for B. Jain Publishers (P) Ltd., D-157, Sector 63, Noida - 201307, U.P.

Registered office: 1921/10, Chuna Mandi, Paharganj, New Delhi-110055

Printed in India at Narain Printers & Binder, Noida

Preface

English Olympiad Book 8 has been carefully written, designed and brought to fruition in the hope that it carries all necessary elements that make each exercise a learning experience for children, their teachers and parents. It also ensures gradual progression from English Olympiad Book 7.

'Learning by doing' - the ethos behind introducing Olympiads is an effort to achieve perfection. In this spirit, we have followed a systematic pattern, inclusive of the scientific method and child-centric approach, wherein each concept has been explained again (as understood that it was done as part of Grammar lessons). Therefore, revisions here leave enough room to substantiate upon experiential learning that help students to deliver better.

In the end, we have also provided five test papers that carry a diverse set of questions. It will help children test themselves amidst all concepts put together in random order, which will bring greater degree of clarity and thought.

Salient Features

- Multiple choice questions
- Use of necessary illustrations to make learning simpler
- Model test papers in the end to make a wholesome assessment
- Inclusion of almost all aspects of English Olympiad exams

We wish all readers of **English Olympiad Book–8** a joyful experience.

Contents

1. Substitution 5
2. Nouns and Pronouns 9
3. Verbs and Phrasal Verbs 14
4. Adverbs and Adjectives 19
5. Articles and Prepositions 24
6. Conjunctions and Determiners 28
7. Meaningful Sentences and Punctuation 31
8. Tenses 34
9. Voices and Narration 37
10. Composition 42
11. Comprehension 45
12. Spoken and Written Expression 51

    Model Test Paper-1 53
    Model Test Paper-2 58
    Model Test Paper-3 62
    Model Test Paper-4 67
    Model Test Paper-5 72

Answer Key 77

SUBSTITUTION

One word that substitutes many words and helps to make a sentence crisp and brief.

For example: A person who cures patients is operating upon my mother.
A doctor is operating upon my mother.

EXERCISE 1

Tick the correct word from the given description.

1. The skill required to manage international affairs
    a) Democracy b) Diplomacy
    c) Tenacity d) Tact

2. Severe scarcity of food
    a) Poverty b) Malnutrition
    c) Shortage d) Famine

3. The science which studies the occult influence of stars on human beings
    a) Physics b) Astronomy
    c) Astrology d) Optics

4. One who has no money
    a) Debtor b) Loser
    c) Wealthy d) Pauper

5. Revolt against the government to bring about complete change
    a) Revolution b) War
    c) Evolution d) Riot

6. Periodical publication of official news
    a) Magazine b) Memo
    c) Gazette d) Newsletter

7. A person who loves mankind and works for their well-being
    a) Philanthropist b) Devotee
    c) Anthropologist d) Trustee

8. **Place where animals like cows and horses are kept**
   a) House b) Sty
   c) Stable d) Kennel

9. **Medical study of skin and its disease**
   a) Endocrinology b) Dermatology
   c) Orthopaedics d) Genealogy

10. **Ready to believe**
    a) Credible b) Incredible
    c) Creditable d) Credulous

11. **Science of birds**
    a) Anthropology b) Palaeontology
    c) Ornithology d) Physiology

12. **One who believes that all things and events in life are predetermined**
    a) Fatalist b) Puritan
    c) Tyrant d) Egoist

13. **Something that relates to everyone in the world**
    a) General b) Universal
    c) Native d) Common

14. **One who hates women**
    a) Womaniser b) Feminist
    c) Misogynist d) Patriot

15. **One who loves one's country**
    a) Patriot b) Martyr
    c) Traitor d) Revolutionary

EXERCISE 2

Choose the correct option to complete the proverbs.

1. **A book holds a house of _____.**
   a) wealth b) gold
   c) diamond d) silver

2. **A day of _____ is longer than a month of joy.**
   a) harmony b) happy
   c) cheerful d) sorrow

3. **A drop of ink may make a million _____.**
   a) think b) read
   c) write d) poem

4. **Better lose the saddle than the _____.**
   a) cat b) sorry
   c) horse d) choice

5. **Better be alone than in bad _____.**
   a) friend b) mood
   c) people d) company

6. **_____ begins at home.**
   a) Charity b) Honesty
   c) Adversity d) Cleanliness

7. **Diamond cuts _____.**
   a) silver b) copper
   c) diamond d) iron

8. **_____ is the mother of good fortune.**
   a) Intelligence b) Diligence
   c) Misfortune d) Wealth

9. **Every man is the _____ of his own fortune.**
   a) master b) creator
   c) judge d) architect

10. **Hard _____ breaks no bones.**
    a) words b) money
    c) work d) weapons

11. **_____ is bliss.**
    a) Misfortune b) Love
    c) Ignorance d) Hard work

12. **The more _____, the less speed.**
    a) haste b) learn
    c) quick d) read

13. **Many _____ make light work.**
    a) works b) people
    c) hands d) boys

EXERCISE 3

Match with the most appropriate meaning of the following.

1. **Money doesn't grow on trees.**

   a) Having lots of money.
   b) There is a money plant.
   c) One should not waste money because it is not plentiful or obtained easily.
   d) There should be no limitations on spending money.

2. **An idle brain is the devil's workshop.**

   a) Thinking of devils
   b) Devils live in brain
   c) Neither good nor bad
   d) When you are busy working you avoid temptation

3. **Don't judge a book by its cover.**

   a) Do not be deceived by appearance
   b) Always check cover before buying a book
   c) Cover depicts the book
   d) Best books have fancy covers

4. **Actions speak louder than words.**

   a) Speak loudly.
   b) What a person actually does is more important than what they say they will do.
   c) Before doing anything always shout.
   d) None of the above

5. **Opportunity seldom knocks twice.**

   a) Always grab the opportunity.
   b) Don't miss opportunities that come along.
   c) Opportunities will come again and again.
   d) Having limitless potentialities.

6. **Punctuality is the soul of business.**

   a) Money is not required for business.
   b) Punctual people can earn name and fame.
   c) You should always be on time for your business appointments.
   d) None of the above

7. **Learn to walk before you run.**

   a) Try to run before you walk.
   b) You must not be too confident.
   c) An occasion that is missed will not come again.
   d) Don't rush into doing something before you know how to do it.

Nouns and Pronouns

Nouns are names of persons, places or things.
A noun is used to identify any class of people, places or things (also called common noun), or to name a particular one of these (also called proper noun).

Pronouns
Pronouns can function as a noun phrase used by itself and that refers either to the participants in the discourse (**for example:** I, you) or to someone or something mentioned elsewhere in the discourse (**for example:** she, it, this).

EXERCISE 1

Choose the correct options to fill in the collective nouns.

1. Rohan bought six glasses of the same kind for the function.
   a) a set of six glasses
   b) a pair of six glasses
   c) a group of six glasses
   d) a stock of six glasses

2. Please take this _____ of old newspapers to the recycle bin.
   a) series
   b) clutch
   c) pile
   d) bundle

3. Look at the exquisite _____ of pearls she is wearing around her neck.
   a) chain
   b) set
   c) string
   d) ring

4. The group of singers at church sang beautifully.
   a) crew
   b) horde
   c) team
   d) choir

5. We need a lot of flowers strung together to decorate the main door.
   a) necklace
   b) wreath
   c) garland
   d) bouquet

6. The people who work at the company are requested to check their mails every day.
   a) servants
   b) workers
   c) employees
   d) labourers

7. **The people working on the ship will return after a month.**
    a) army b) group
    c) troupe d) crew

8. **A giant lot of dust is moving towards the city.**
    a) pile of dust b) storm of dust
    c) cloud of dust d) heap of dust.

EXERCISE 2

Which is the correct abstract noun in the given sentences?

1. **As a child, I loved to play music.**
    a) child b) loved
    c) play d) music

2. **One must always tell the truth.**
    a) one b) tell
    c) always d) truth

3. **Bravery awards are given every year to five children.**
    a) bravery b) children
    c) five d) given

4. **He is known for inviting troubles.**
    a) inviting b) known
    c) he d) troubles

5. **The growth of a country depends entirely on its people.**
    a) country b) people
    c) entirely d) growth

EXERCISE 3

Fill in the blanks with the correct form of nouns.

1. **His _____ was no different from yours.**
    a) sons b) daughters
    c) children d) childhood

2. **It's always a great _____ to see the Taj Mahal.**
    a) pleasure b) please
    c) pleasant d) pleased

3. The _____ of the rope is still not appropriate.
    a) long b) length
    c) longer d) longs

4. Think with _____ before taking any action.
    a) wise b) wisdom
    c) brain d) mind

5. There is a _____ in my company if you are interested.
    a) vacant b) empty
    c) emptiness d) vacancy

6. No matter how long it takes, _____ will be served.
    a) judgment b) justice
    c) judge d) judgement

EXERCISE 4

Fill in the blanks using indefinite pronouns.

1. _____ of the people on the road came ahead.
    a) No b) No one
    c) Nobody d) None

2. _____ hardly knows what to do.
    a) They b) We
    c) Her d) One

3. _____ entered the house in our absence.
    a) Someone b) Everybody
    c) Anybody d) Anyone

4. Out of many people, only a _____ left early.
    a) many b) much
    c) few d) more

5. _____ believe in ghosts; some don't.
    a) Some b) Any
    c) No d) All

EXERCISE 5

Fill in the blanks with the correct pronouns.

1. He has never been to the country where _____ parents were born.
   a) he			b) she
   c) her			d) his

2. Between you and _____, I don't trust him.
   a) I			b) you
   c) he			d) me

3. It's up to _____ what he wants to do.
   a) his			b) hers
   c) we			d) him

4. This is the boy _____ saved her from drowning.
   a) he			b) she
   c) her			d) who

5. First let them get to know _____.
   a) herself		b) himself
   c) themselves		d) each other

6. The car cannot come here all by _____.
   a) herself		b) himself
   c) themselves		d) itself

7. The bike _____ was stolen yesterday has been found.
   a) it			b) what
   c) where			d) which

8. I know somebody _____ can repair the fan.
   a) whom			b) he
   c) she			d) who

9. I don't like _____ who talk too much.
   a) them			b) these
   c) those			d) you

10. I must catch the bus _____ leaves at 6.
    a) it			b) who
    c) that			d) one

EXERCISE 6

Choose the correct pronoun.

1. The girls are playing in the garden. _____ look very happy.
   a) He
   b) She
   c) All
   d) They

2. The boys are making a lot of noise. Please ask _____ to be quiet.
   a) him
   b) those
   c) them
   d) they

3. Where is Rohan? I haven't seen _____ in several days.
   a) him
   b) you
   c) her
   d) all

4. Raju complained to the teacher. _____ bicycle had been stolen.
   a) Our
   b) My
   c) Your
   d) His

5. My neighbours are some students. _____ are very noisy.
   a) Them
   b) They
   c) He
   d) I

VERBS AND PHRASAL VERBS

A **verb** is used to describe an action, state, or occurrence, and forms the main part of the predicate of a sentence, such as hear or happen.

A **phrasal verb** is an idiomatic phrase consisting of a verb and another element, typically either an adverb, as in break down, or a preposition, for example see to, or a combination of both, such as look down on.

EXERCISE 1

Fill in the blanks correctly.

1. _____ you like more cheese on the sandwich?
   a) Must   b) Could
   c) Would   d) Have to

2. You _____ eat more vegetables.
   a) should   b) might
   c) may   d) could

3. I _____ like to buy the same television for my house.
   a) could   b) would
   c) must   d) have to

4. _____ I have a cup of coffee please?
   a) Must   b) Might
   c) May   d) Would

5. You _____ burst crackers near children.
   a) have to   b) may
   c) shouldn't   d) couldn't

6. The passengers _____ wear their seatbelts throughout the flight, if they want.
   a) could   b) must
   c) can   d) may

7. We _____ go to the concert if the rain stops. We are not sure.
   a) mustn't   b) might
   c) have to   d) wouldn't

14

8. I _____ ice skate very well.
   a) can			b) may
   c) must			d) should

9. The boys _____ wake up before 7:30 am. They have a class at 8:00 am.
   a) would			b) can't
   c) could			d) have to

10. The rock band _____ play very well last year. Now they are much better.
    a) must			b) couldn't
    c) can			d) should

11. He _____ around the filthy room in distaste.
    a) looked			b) looking
    c) am looks			d) is looks

12. I promised Sam that I _____ go to the hockey game with him on Friday.
    a) will			b) had to
    c) must			d) would

13. The test starts at 1:00pm. We_____ return before that.
    a) must			b) ought
    c) can			d) should

14. Wait for me at home until I _____ from office.
    a) returned			b) am return
    c) returns			d) return

15. They _____ asked to give opinion in their own words.
    a) maybe			b) should be
    c) might			d) have being

EXERCISE 2

Choose the correct option and fill in the blanks.

1. I painted the house and it _____ out better than I expected.
   a) had turned			b) would have turned
   c) turns			d) turned

2. I _____ for a swim but I changed my mind.
   a) wasn't going to go		b) won't go to
   c) isn't going to		d) wasn't going

3. I don't remember _____ this computer.
   a) how long I've had
   b) when did I get
   c) for how long have I had
   d) when I was getting

4. The newspaper says _____.
   a) it would rain
   b) it had rained
   c) it would have rained
   d) it will rain

5. Roger _____ the course you are telling about.
   a) had already taken
   b) has already taken
   c) took already
   d) would have already taken

6. _____ the new phone you bought?
   a) How big is
   b) How big it is
   c) It is big
   d) Is it big

7. Ved was just going to bed when his father _____ from work.
   a) is going
   b) is coming
   c) had come home
   d) came home

8. You should _____ your shoes.
   a) brought
   b) had brought
   c) to bring
   d) have brought

9. Ginni _____ have kicked the poor dog; now it is howling.
   a) must not
   b) should not
   c) could not
   d) cannot

10. Mayank _____ decide what to get his mother for her birthday.
    a) could not
    b) might not
    c) should not
    d) may not

EXERCISE 3

Fill in the blanks with suitable phrasal verbs.

1. We need to _____ our expenses as the prices of goods are going up.
   a) get on with
   b) go on with
   c) cut down on
   d) keep out of

2. Nate was surprised to _____ his room after the narrow escape.
   a) get on with
   b) wake up in
   c) coming out on
   d) hung up on

3. It was just his luck that in his first, he is _____ last year's champion.
   a) up against   b) out in open
   c) keep out of   d) snap out of

4. That rude manager _____ me in the middle of the phone call.
   a) snap out of   b) went up against
   c) check in on   d) hung up on

5. Everything _____ 340 rupees.
   a) hung up on   b) get on with
   c) coming out on   d) adds up to

6. I will _____ you in the evening again.
   a) coming out on   b) check in on
   c) wake up in   d) went up against

7. The test results are _____ this Friday.
   a) check in on   b) coming out on
   c) cut down on   d) keep out of

8. Please _____ this matter.
   a) wake up in   b) check in on
   c) cut down on   d) stay out of

EXERCISE 4

Replace the underlined words with the correct option.

1. We need to **think of** a plan before it's too late.
   a) come in to   b) come up with
   c) come upon with   d) come away with

2. We are **dining out** tonight.
   a) renting out   b) staying out
   c) eating out   d) going out

3. Before you go on with the story, let me add **something**.
   a) relay   b) retain
   c) board   d) continue

4. Rohan will not **stand for** this sort of disrespect.
   a) indulge   b) involve
   c) ignore   d) tolerate

5. **I think that man looks like my uncle.**

    a) appears
    b) mimics
    c) resembles
    d) familiarises

6. **Ankita accidentally saw a copy of your offer letter.**

    a) looked over
    b) read through
    c) skimmed across
    d) glanced upon

7. **Sumit called off the trip when he came to know that his parents were coming.**

    a) deleted
    b) engaged
    c) cancelled
    d) reported

8. **Mahesh has been putting off his plans for a long time.**

    a) reacting
    b) cutting
    c) delaying
    d) shifting

9. **It all boils down to what you decide.**

    a) relates to
    b) transfers to
    c) omits to
    d) depends on

10. **Ankur and Anuj finally made up after Aashi spoke to both of them.**

    a) reunited
    b) reconciled
    c) joined
    d) merged

ADVERBS AND ADJECTIVES

4

An **adverb** is a word that describes or modifies a verb, an adjective or another adverb. For example: quickly, slowly, gently

An **adjective** is a descriptive word that describes a noun (pretty, happy, silly, sunny).

EXERCISE 1

Choose the most suitable adverb to complete the sentences.

1. **She laughed _____ when she heard the news.**
   a) furiously   b) heavily
   c) happily   d) foolishly

2. **They listened _____ to the instructions.**
   a) carefully   b) consciously
   c) clearly   d) smoothly

3. **They walked _____ along the beach.**
   a) nicely   b) seriously
   c) slowly   d) patiently

4. **They lived as _____ as possible to keep their expenses down.**
   a) smartly   b) poorly
   c) cheaply   d) casually

5. **They cheered _____ for their team, urging them to do better.**
   a) sensibly   b) enthusiastically
   c) gladly   d) angrily

6. **The students worked _____ for the examination.**
   a) sincerely   b) feverishly
   c) patiently   d) normally

7. **Dr Banerjee ____ dressed the wound, causing as little pain as possible.**
   a) strongly   b) thoughtfully
   c) gracefully   d) gently

19

8. The demonstrators shouted _____, demanding that their boss meet them.
   a) angrily   b) seriously
   c) gaily   d) lazily

9. Visitors to the open house were _____ greeted by the host.
   a) hastily   b) truly
   c) warmly   d) highly

10. The magician _____ demonstrated his skill to the audience.
    a) cleverly   b) wildly
    c) patiently   d) foolishly

EXERCISE 2

Fill in the blanks with the most suitable adverb.

1. I _____ go to bed at 10 o'clock. (frequency)
   a) occasionally   b) usually
   c) clearly   d) once

2. I have _____ been to the USA. (frequency)
   a) sometimes   b) mostly
   c) rarely   d) very

3. I _____ use extra salt in my food. (frequency)
   a) rarely   b) occasionally
   c) clearly   d) sometimes

4. I was _____ impressed with her performance. (degree)
   a) once   b) mostly
   c) often   d) very

5. I _____ go for a walk in the park. (frequency)
   a) very   b) occasionally
   c) sometimes   d) usually

6. I have been to Australia just _____. (frequency)
   a) most   b) more
   c) once   d) much

7. I _____ take a bath before I go to bed. (frequency)
   a) fairly   b) always
   c) much   d) nearly

8. My grandparents live in Kerala. I visit them _____. (frequency)
    a) scarcely b) too
    c) clearly d) often

9. I watch English films _____. (frequency)
    a) always b) enough
    c) clearly d) occasionally

10. They _____ go out. (frequency)
    a) very b) quickly
    c) slowly d) hardly

EXERCISE 3

Choose the correct answer and fill in the blanks.

1. The crowd was _____ when the home team scored in the last few seconds.
    a) spirited b) flustered
    c) glad d) thrilled

2. He appeared _____ during the interview and was not able to respond well.
    a) nervous b) serene
    c) downcast d) submissive

3. She may be a good worker but that does not necessarily make her a _____ manager.
    a) competent b) compliant
    c) competitive d) composed

4. His work was so _____ that the teacher asked him to do it again.
    a) sloppy b) notorious
    c) devious d) sullen

5. The _____ and strong man helped them lift the heavy case onto the truck.
    a) stout b) feeble
    c) willowy d) skinny

6. He is _____ because there is nothing interesting to do.
    a) boring b) bored
    c) indifferent d) jubilant

7. The _____ girl hid herself under the bed.
    a) scared b) sacred
    c) excited d) exciting

8. You should not be too _____ on yourself. Just don't make the same mistake again.
   a) harsh   b) stern
   c) frantic   d) placid

9. She was _____ after to know that her handbag had been found.
   a) depressed   b) weary
   c) flighty   d) relieved

10. She has the _____ task of taking the distinguished guest on a tour to Jaipur.
    a) arrogant   b) enviable
    c) placid   d) peaceable

11. The _____ pupil was punished by his teacher.
    a) misleading   b) mischievous
    c) mysterious   d) missing

12. The hospital received a big donation from the _____ businessman.
    a) callous   b) righteous
    c) caring   d) generous

13. We noticed that she was _____ when Douglas did not give her a birthday gift.
    a) unpleasant   b) displeased
    c) insincere   d) demure

14. She was _____ by the adults and did not dare to say a word.
    a) intimidated   b) inept
    c) disgruntled   d) discontented

15. Carol has a _____ interest in collecting stamps.
    a) sharp   b) tense
    c) keen   d) sensible

16. They were _____ after losing the game.
    a) dejected   b) ejected
    c) subjected   d) objected

17. She looked _____ although she had been working for more than 10 hours.
    a) fatigued   b) fresh
    c) complacent   d) jaded

22

18. He was _____ and apologised to his parents for his wrong doings.

   a) zealous
   b) frantic
   c) fervent
   d) remorseful

19. The teacher was too _____ towards the class.

   a) incompetent
   b) lenient
   c) humble
   d) demure

20. You will have to be more _____ in order to get the best out of them.

   a) flexible
   b) capable
   c) disabled
   d) incapable

ARTICLES AND PREPOSITIONS

5

An **article** is a word used to modify a noun, which is a person, place, object or idea.

For example: a, an, the.

A **preposition** is a word or set of words that indicates location (in, near, beside, on top of) or some other relationship between a noun or pronoun and other parts of the sentence (about, after, besides, instead of, in accordance with).

EXERCISE 1

Choose the correct set of articles and complete the sentences.

1. **Sandeep is _____ tennis coach. He teaches tennis to _____ students of my school. He is _____ extremely good coach.**

   a) a, the, an
   c) the, an, a
   b) a, an, the
   d) an, the, a

2. **He is _____ very strange man. He has _____ queer habit of sleeping during _____ day and remaining awake during _____ night.**

   a) a, the, an, a
   c) the, an, a, the
   b) a, an, the, a
   d) a, a, the, the

3. **While _____ family was away, some burglars broke into _____ house and ransacked. They ran away with all _____ jewellery.**

   a) a, the, an
   c) the, the, a
   b) a, an, a
   d) the, the, the

4. **Our maid comes to our house thrice _____ week. Apart from washing _____ clothes, she sometimes also cleans _____ house. She is paid two thousand rupees _____ month.**

   a) a, the, an, a
   c) a, the, the, a
   b) a, an, the, a
   d) a, a, the, the

5. **As I was walking along _____ sandy beach, I spotted _____ bottle floating in _____ sea. I picked up _____ bottle and found _____ note in it.**

   a) a, a, the, the, a
   c) a, a, the, the, a
   b) the, an, a, the, the
   d) the, a, a, the, an

24

6. **Rishav has always been interested in cooking. He is currently undergoing training in _____ hotel overseas. He plans to be _____ chef and open up his own restaurant.**

   a) a, a
   b) a, an
   c) an, a
   d) the, a

7. **_____ four men involved in _____ kidnap attempt are wanted by _____ police. _____ reward for information leading to their arrest is five lakh rupees.**

   a) The, the, the, The
   b) A, a, a, A
   c) An, an, an, An,
   d) A, a, an, An,

8. **_____ tourism industry in _____ country is indeed booming. As _____ result, many young people are enrolling in tourism-related courses.**

   a) The, the, a
   b) A, the, an
   c) A, an, a
   d) The, a, the

9. **Are you still interested in buying _____ car? I saw _____ sedan in _____ showroom next to my office. _____ price is also very reasonable.**

   a) the, the, a, an
   b) a, the, an, the
   c) a, an, a, the
   d) a, a, the, the

10. **Sneha recently applied for _____ job in _____ hotel in Mumbai. Just yesterday, she received _____ letter from them.**

    a) a, a, a
    b) the, a, an
    c) a, an, the
    d) a, the, a

11. **Have you ever seen _____ snow before?**

    a) a
    b) the
    c) an
    d) no article needed

12. **_____ National Library is having _____ special week of activities.**

    a) a, a
    b) a, an
    c) an, a
    d) the, a

13. **Although he was poor, _____ man returned the suitcase full of money to its owner.**

    a) the
    b) an
    c) a
    d) no article needed

14. **We enjoy _____ music played by this new band. _____ band plays very well.**

    a) a, The
    b) the, A
    c) the, The
    d) an, The

15. Will you please answer _____ phone? I'm busy in _____ kitchen.
   a) a, the
   b) the, a
   c) the, the
   d) an, the

EXERCISE 2

Choose the correct preposition to fill in the blanks.

1. I stayed _____ at the office last night because there was a power cut in my colony.
   a) out
   b) from
   c) as
   d) over

2. _____ my opinion, she should be given another chance.
   a) Along
   b) In
   c) Through
   d) On

3. It was very kind _____ you to visit.
   a) with
   b) for
   c) of
   d) after

4. Can you look _____ my dog when I am out of town?
   a) from
   b) out
   c) along
   d) after

5. Go _____ those stairs. His room is the third door on the left.
   a) up
   b) to
   c) over
   d) at

EXERCISE 3

Choose the correct preposition to complete the passage.

The chameleon is found (1) _____ Africa and Madagascar. It can also be found (2) _____ some parts of Asia and southern Europe. Some varieties of chameleons can grow (3) _____ a length of 60 centimetres. However, the most common variety grows to around 30 centimetres. The amazing thing (4) _____ the chameleon is that it can change its colour. It is capable of changing quickly (5) _____ white to yellow, black, green or brown. It is able to do this because of the variation (6) _____ light and temperature of the surroundings. The chameleon lives in trees. Its tail and feet can hold on (7) _____ the branches while it is reaching (8) _____ to catch its prey. It can remain very still (9) _____ a branch (10) _____ hours.

1. a) in   b) to   c) out   d) on
2. a) to   b) in   c) out   d) on
3. a) out   b) on   c) in   d) to
4. a) from   b) about   c) to   d) in
5. a) about   b) from   c) in   d) out
6. a) on   b) out   c) to   d) in
7. a) out   b) to   c) in   d) on
8. a) about   b) out   c) for   d) from
9. a) on   b) out   c) to   d) in
10. a) out   b) about   c) for   d) from

Conjunctions and Determiners

A **conjunction** is a part of speech that connects words, phrases or clauses.
For example: and, or.

A modifying word that **determines** the kind of reference a noun or noun group has.
For example: a, the, some, much, every.

EXERCISE 1

Complete the sentences using the correct options.

1. _____ it continues to rain heavily, the match will be postponed.
   a) After b) When
   c) If d) Although

2. The thief ran away _____ the policemen arrived.
   a) before b) If
   c) because d) although

3. I try to eat less fast food _____ it is not very nutritional.
   a) when b) if
   c) because d) although

4. We talked softly and turned the music down _____ we saw the baby sleeping.
   a) if b) because
   c) although d) when

5. My twin brother loves sports, _____ I am hopeless in all games.
   a) but b) so
   c) because d) when

6. Fatimah saw a strange man following her _____ she ran to the nearest police station.
   a) and b) but
   c) so d) or

7. He is old _____ he is still active.
   a) and b) but
   c) so d) if

8. Mr Chandra could not recognise me _____ he has not seen me for three years.

   a) if
   b) as
   c) so
   d) but

9. You can _____ wear the cotton pyjamas _____ the silk pyjamas.

   a) either, or
   b) or, nor
   c) both, and
   d) but, still

10. _____ he did not sleep well last night, he insisted on going to work.

    a) Since
    b) Although
    c) Though
    d) As

11. You have to wait _____ midnight before you can open your birthday gift.

    a) until
    b) since
    c) despite
    d) because

12. You will have to pick one of the dresses here _____ you will not have anything nice to wear to the party tomorrow.

    a) even though
    b) despite
    c) or else
    d) since

EXERCISE 2

Fill in the blanks with appropriate determiners.

1. Use _____ ink-remover to get the stains off your shirt.

   a) many
   b) much
   c) a few
   d) a little

2. We must bring _____ food to last us the whole week.

   a) enough
   b) little
   c) much
   d) many

3. I don't have _____ experience in work of this sort.

   a) some
   b) many
   c) a little
   d) any

4. I have only _____ sugar left. It isn't enough to sweeten the drink.

   a) many
   b) much
   c) a few
   d) a little

5. There is _____ rice in the pot. So eat as much as you can.
   a) a little   b) many
   c) some   d) plenty of

6. Let's do _____ shopping while we're in town.
   a) much   b) many
   c) some   d) any

7. "Will 10 dollars do? Is that _____ for you?" his father asked.
   a) many   b) much
   c) enough   d) plenty of

8. She had _____ work to do than anyone else.
   a) many   b) more
   c) plenty of   d) some

9. "Oh dear!" she said, "the _____ money I earn, the _____ I save."
   a) much, few   b) more, less
   c) enough, some   d) plenty of, little

10. I admit that I don't have _____ knowledge on the subject. I'll have to spend _____ time reading up.
    a) many, more   b) much, extra
    c) much, more   d) plenty of, lot of

11. There isn't _____ improvement in his health. He is still very weak.
    a) more   b) much
    c) many   d) plenty of

12. Is there _____ bread here for all of you? If there isn't, I'll go and buy _____ more.
    a) few, little   b) any, little
    c) enough, some   d) any, some

13. Lily spilt _____ ink on the floor, but made _____ effort to clean up the stain.
    a) some, lot   b) some, no
    c) enough, no   d) much, no

14. Don't add _____ salt. I have already put in _____ and the soup tastes just right.
    a) more, enough   b) plenty of, some
    c) some, lot   d) enough, more

30

Meaningful Sentences and Punctuation

EXERCISE 1

Choose the grammatically correct, meaningful sentences from the given options.

1. a) Below eight children not are allowed.
   b) Children not are below eight allowed.
   c) Allowed are not children below eight.
   d) Children below eight are not allowed.

2. a) Would no like sight one to such see a.
   b) One to such see a would no like sight.
   c) Such see a would no like sight one to.
   d) No one would like to see such a sight.

3. a) Hardworking children always succeed.
   b) Always hardworking succeed children.
   c) Succeed always children hardworking.
   d) Children succeed always hardworking.

4. a) Dress on this beautiful looks you.
   b) Beautiful looks you dress on this.
   c) This dress looks beautiful on you.
   d) You on beautiful looks dress this.

5. a) Required assistants are shop at the.
   b) Assistants are required at the shop.
   c) Shop the at required are assistants.
   d) The at shop are assistants required.

6. a) Money you me lend can some?
   b) Some can lend me you money?
   c) Can you lend me some money?
   d) Money you me lend some can?

7. a) Chinese served Italian are here meals and.
   b) Chinese and Italian meals are served here.
   c) Are here meals and Chinese served Italian.
   d) Meals and Chinese served Italian are here.

8.   a) Are cinnamon benefits what the of?
       b) Benefits what the of are cinnamon?
       c) What the of are cinnamon benefits?
       d) What are the benefits of cinnamon?

9.   a) Was clever Birbal extremely witty and.
       b) Birbal was extremely clever and witty.
       c) Birbal extremely witty clever was and.
       d) Birbal extremely witty and was clever.

10.   a) My bag lost in I train the.
       b) Lost in I train the my bag.
       c) I lost my bag in the train.
       d) The my bag lost in I train.

EXERCISE 2

Choose the correctly punctuated sentences.

1.   a) The planet nearest to the sun is Mercury.
       b) the Planet nearest to the Sun is Mercury.
       c) The Planet nearest to the Sun is Mercury.
       d) The planet nearest to the Sun is Mercury.

2.   a) I have taken notes from your book however I still have questions.
       b) I have taken notes from your book, however I still have questions.
       c) I have taken notes from your book; however, I still have questions.
       d) I have taken notes from your book however; I still have questions.

3.   a) Can we meet tomorrow at 10 30?
       b) Can we meet tomorrow at 10:30?
       c) Can we meet tomorrow at 1030.
       d) Can we meet tomorrow at 10,30?

4.   a) Dear Mr. Williams,
       b) Dear Mr. Williams;
       c) Dear Mr. Williams:
       d) dear Mr Williams.

5.   a) Why don't we get together to watch the Cricket world cup!
       b) why don't we get together to watch the cricket world cup.
       c) Why don't we get together to watch the Cricket World Cup?
       d) why don't we get together to watch the cricket World Cup?

6.   a) Everyone has special skills and some people use them very well.
       b) Everyone has special skills; and some people use them very well.
       c) Everyone has special skills and, some people use them very well.
       d) Everyone has special skills; and, some people use them very well.

7. a) We can try to find it now, or we can wait until it's lighter.
    b) We can try to find it, now or we can wait until its lighter.
    c) We can try to find it now or, we can wait until it's lighter.
    d) We can try, to find it now, or we can wait, until it's lighter.

8. a) You're going to come to my party right?
    b) Your going to come to my party right?
    c) You're going to come to my party, right.
    d) You're going to come to my party, right?

9. a) In addition to putting your name on your paper please add the Date.
    b) In addition to putting your Name on your paper please add the date.
    c) In addition to putting your name on your paper, please add the date.
    d) in addition to putting your name on your paper, please add the date.

10. a) When you are done eating, clear your place
    b) when you are done Eating, clear your place.
    c) When you are done eating, clear your Place.
    d) When you are done eating, clear your place.

11. a) Shell never get her own room if she can't keep it clean.
    b) She'll never get her own Room if she can't keep it clean.
    c) She'll never get her own room if she can't keep it clean.
    d) she'll never get her own room if she cant keep it clean.

12. a) Harry announced, "The library is closing in 15 minutes."
    b) Harry announced "The library is closing in 15 minutes."
    c) Harry announced The library is closing in 15 minutes."
    d) Harry announced "The library is closing in 15 minutes."

13. a) On April 14, 2012, our school held its centennial.
    b) On April 14, 2012 our school held its centennial.
    c) On April 14, 2012 our school, held its centennial.
    d) On April 14 2012, our school held its centennial.

14. a) "That," We were informed, "Is a snow leopard."
    b) "That," we were informed, "is a snow leopard."
    c) "That," We were informed, "is a snow leopard."
    d) "That," we were informed, "Is a snow leopard."

15. a) Naina baked the cake, set the table, and, decorated the house.
    b) Naina baked the cake, set the table and, decorated the house.
    c) Naina baked the cake, set the table and decorated the house.
    d) Naina baked the cake, set the table, and decorated the house.

Tenses

EXERCISE 1

Fill in the blanks with the correct tense forms.

1. _____ these pants belong to Regina?
   a) Is   b) Are
   c) Do   d) Does

2. _____ you all right? You look a little pale.
   a) Is   b) Are
   c) Do   d) Does

3. Being rude to Mr Hassan in front of her guests at the party last night _____ too much.
   a) was   b) are
   c) is   d) were

4. The athlete _____ by the time I reached the track.
   a) was running   b) ran
   c) will run   d) run

5. He _____ the rails and got on his motorcycle to make his getaway.
   a) jumped over   b) are jumping
   c) jumps   d) will jump

6. Even though she is working in New York, she _____ back and forth during the weekend to spend time with her family.
   a) fly   b) flown
   c) flies   d) was flying

7. I _____ a question for you. Why are you dressed like a pirate?
   a) have   b) has
   c) had   d) am having

8. She _____ the children to class an hour ago.
   a) taken   b) has taken
   c) took   d) are taking

9. He _____ to take the job in Chicago. He will head to the office to sign the paperwork required.

   a) decided
   b) deciding
   c) decide
   d) has decided

10. _____ this Mr Smith's house?

    a) Were
    b) Are
    c) Am
    d) Is

11. Right now, the police officers _____ combing the area.

    a) were
    b) are
    c) is
    d) was

12. He _____ not taken bath today.

    a) has
    b) had
    c) have
    d) have had

13. Sneha has not started working yet, so she _____ not spend money carelessly.

    a) do
    b) did
    c) does
    d) doing

14. I am having a backache. I need someone to help me _____ my back.

    a) is rubbing
    b) rubbed
    c) will rub
    d) rub

15. The rabbit _____ all the way and entered the hole. I was hoping to catch it.

    a) hops
    b) had hopped
    c) will hop
    d) is hopping

16. We _____ from Amber. She is looking for us.

    a) are hiding
    b) hid
    c) hide
    d) hidden

17. Anthony and Sonia _____ in a small ceremony in the garden of their new home next month.

    a) married
    b) marries
    c) will marry
    d) marry

18. Amazing! He _____ the names of all the people who had voted in his favour.

    a) memorising
    b) memorise
    c) will memorise
    d) memorised

19. He _____ a struggling actor by day and a guard at night.
    a) was   b) are
    c) am   d) were

20. _____ you see that? There was a bright light above the stadium over there. I saw it!
    a) Did   b) Do
    c) Done   d) Doing

21. "I _____ the next train out. I'll see you in half an hour," Ria said to her friends at the mall.
    a) is catching   b) am catching
    c) was catching   d) are catching

22. "I _____ the state of the walls in the school very disturbing. The structure may collapse anytime," said the contractor.
    a) founded   b) find
    c) is finding   d) finds

23. Lena _____ on her way to her grandmother's cottage when she was followed by the wolf.
    a) was   b) are
    c) is   d) were

24. I was not _____ but I couldn't sleep because of the smell of the mosquito repellent.
    a) bite   b) bitten
    c) bit   d) biting

25. Silence please! They _____ in the midst of deciding who will win the pageant.
    a) was   b) are
    c) am   d) were

Voices and Narration

EXERCISE 1

Fill in the blanks to complete the sentences.

1. Good performance _____ shown by him.
   a) is been
   b) has been
   c) has be
   d) has

2. The match _____ by my friends.
   a) has watched
   b) is being watched
   c) are watching
   d) watched

3. This matter _____ by you.
   a) is looked into
   b) looked into
   c) to be looked into
   d) should be looked into

4. A house _____ by them next to our school.
   a) is built
   b) being built
   c) to be built
   d) is being built

5. I _____ by somebody about the fair in the town.
   a) am told
   b) will be told
   c) told
   d) was told

6. The last day's play between India and Australia _____ by rain.
   a) is disrupted
   b) disrupted
   c) has disrupted
   d) was being disrupted

7. She _____ a bull dog by someone.
   a) will given
   b) give
   c) will give
   d) was given

8. The dance was _____ by most of the students.
   a) not enjoy
   b) can't enjoy
   c) not enjoyed
   d) don't enjoy

EXERCISE 2

Choose the active or passive voice of the given sentences.

1. **Do you imitate others?**

   a) Are others imitated by you?
   b) Are others being imitated by you?
   c) Were others being imitated by you?
   d) Have others been imitated by you?

2. **When I saw her, she was crossing the road.**

   a) When she seen by me, she was crossing the road.
   b) When she was being seen by me, she was crossing the road.
   c) When she was seen by me, she was crossing the road.
   d) When she saw by me, she was crossing the road.

3. **Who will lead the nation in such crisis?**

   a) By whom will the nation be led in such crisis?
   b) By whom will the nation led in such crisis?
   c) By whom will the nation been led in such crisis?
   d) By whom would the nation be led in such crisis?

4. **Why does she always make lame excuses?**

   a) Why lame excuses always made by her?
   b) Why is lame excuses always made by her?
   c) Why do lame excuses always made by her?
   d) Why are lame excuses always made by her?

5. **You have to finish this work as soon as you can.**

   a) This work has been finished by you as soon as you can.
   b) This work has be finished by you as soon as you can.
   c) This work had to finished by you as soon as you can.
   d) This work has to be finished by you as soon as you can.

6. **My teacher asked me to learn the lesson by heart.**

   a) I asked by my teacher to learn the lesson by heart.
   b) I am asked by my teacher to learn the lesson by heart.
   c) I am being asked by my teacher to learn the lesson by heart.
   d) I was asked by my teacher to learn the lesson by heart.

7. **Lion does not eat grass, however hungry he may be.**

   a) Grass is not eaten by a lion, however hungry he may be.
   b) Grass was being not eaten by a lion, however hungry he may be.
   c) Grass is eaten not by a lion, however hungry he may be.
   d) Grass is not being eaten by a lion, however hungry he may be.

8. **Why did you not agree to my proposal?**

   a) Why was my proposal not agreed to?
   b) Why was my proposal not agreed by you?
   c) Why my proposal was not agreed to by you?
   d) Why was my proposal not agreed to by you?

9. **The noise of traffic kept me awake.**

   a) I was kept awake by the noise of the traffic.
   b) The traffic kept me awake by noise.
   c) I kept myself awake due to the noise of the traffic.
   d) I remained awake by the noise of the traffic.

10. **He was congratulated by his teacher on his brilliant success in the recent examination.**

    a) He congratulated his teacher on his brilliant success in the examination.
    b) His teacher congratulated him for his brilliant success in the recent examination.
    c) His teacher congratulated him by his brilliant success in the examination.
    d) His teacher congratulated him.

11. **Who gave you the permission to enter?**

    a) By whom were you given the permission to enter?
    b) By whom was you given the permission to enter?
    c) By whom you were given the permission to enter?
    d) By whom were given you the permission to enter?

12. **Before festivals the shops are thronged with men, women and children.**

    a) During festival people throng the shops.
    b) Men, women and children throng the shops before festivals.
    c) Men, women and children make purchases during festivals.
    d) The shops are thronged by people making purchases.

EXERCISE 3

Change the following sentences to direct or indirect form.

1. **Rohan said, "We passed by a beautiful lake when we went on a trip to Goa."**

   a) Rohan said that they had passed by a beautiful lake when they had gone on a trip to Goa.
   b) Rohan said that they had passed by a beautiful lake when they went on a trip to Goa.
   c) Rohan said that they passed by a beautiful lake when they had gone on a trip to Goa.
   d) Rohan said they passed by a beautiful lake when they went on a trip to Goa.

2. **I said to him, "Why are you working so hard?"**

   a) I asked him why he had been working so hard.
   b) I asked him why he was working so hard.
   c) I asked him why had he been working so hard.
   d) I asked him why was he working so hard.

3. "What about going for a swim? It's quite fine now," he asked me.

   a) He proposed going for a swim as it was quite fine.
   b) He advised to me go for a swim as it was quite fine.
   c) He suggested going for a swim as it was quite fine.
   d) He asked me what about going for a swim as it was quite fine then.

4. David said to Anna, "Mona will leave for her holiday tomorrow."

   a) David told to Anna that Mona would be leaving for her holiday tomorrow.
   b) David told Anna that Mona will leave for her holiday tomorrow.
   c) David told Anna that Mona left for her holiday the next day.
   d) David told Anna that Mona would leave for her holiday the next day.

5. He said to the interviewer, "Could you please repeat the question?"

   a) He requested the interviewer if he could repeat the question.
   b) He requested the interviewer if he could please repeat the question.
   c) He requested the interviewer to please repeat the question.
   d) He requested the interviewer to repeat the question.

6. The father warned his son that he should beware of him.

   a) The father warned his son, "Beware of him!"
   b) The father warned his son, "Watch that chap!"
   c) The father warned his son, "Be careful about him."
   d) The father warned his son, "Don't fall into the trap."

7. "Where will you be tomorrow," I said, "in case I have to ring you?"

   a) I asked where you will be the next day in case I will ring him.
   b) I enquired about his where about the next day in case I would have to ring up.
   c) I asked where he would be the next day in case I had to ring him.
   d) I said to him where he will be in case I have to ring him.

8. Farhan asked Geeta, "Could you lend me a hundred rupees until tomorrow?"

   a) Farhan asked Geeta whether she could lend him a hundred rupees until tomorrow.
   b) Farhan asked Geeta whether she could lend him a hundred rupees until the next day.
   c) Farhan asked Geeta whether she could lend me a hundred rupees until the next day.
   d) Farhan asked whether Geeta could lend me a hundred rupees until the next day.

9. Manya asked Rohan, "Have you sat in an aeroplane before?"

   a) Manya asked Rohan if he has ever sat in an aeroplane.
   b) Manya asked Rohan whether he had sat in an aeroplane earlier.
   c) Manya asked Rohan had he sat in an aeroplane before.
   d) Manya asked Rohan if he sat on an aeroplane before.

10. **Sanjay said to me, "If I hear any news, I'll call you."**

a) Sanjay told me that if he heard any news, he would call me.
b) Sanjay told me that if he heard any new, he will call me.
c) Sanjay told me that if he will hear any news, he will call me.
d) Sanjay told me if he had heard any news, he would call me.

11. **The principal said to Gagan, "Congratulations! Wish you success in life."**

a) The principal wished congratulations and success in life to Gagan.
b) The principal congratulated Gagan and said with you success in life.
c) The principal said congratulations to Gagan and wished him success in life.
d) The principal to congratulated Gagan and wished him success in life.

12. **"Are you alone, my son?" asked a soft voice close behind me.**

a) A soft voice from my back asked if I was alone.
b) A soft voice asked that what I was doing there alone.
c) A soft voice behind me asked if I was alone.
d) A soft voice said to me are you alone son.

13. **The boy said, "Who dare call me a thief?"**

a) The boy told that who dared call him a thief.
b) The boy enquired who dared call him a thief.
c) The boy asked who had dared to call him a thief.
d) The boy wondered who dared call a thief.

14. **John asked, "How long will it take to travel from Germany to South Africa?"**

a) John asked how long it would it take to travel from Germany to South Africa.
b) John asked how long it would take to travel from Germany to South Africa.
c) John asked how long it will take to travel from Germany to South Africa.
d) John asking how long must it take to travel from Germany to South Africa.

15. **Nita ordered her servant to bring her a cup of tea.**

a) Nita told her servant, "Bring her that cup of tea."
b) Nita told her servant, "Bring a cup of tea."
c) Nita said, "Bring me a cup of tea."
d) Nita said to her servant, "Bring me a cup of tea."

Composition

EXERCISE 1

Choose the correct option and then complete the following notice by filling the blanks correctly.

Golden International School

(1) _____

(2) _____

(3) _____

Environment Day is being (4) _____ by the Environment Club on 25th June. There will be poster designing on the (5) _____ of environment and (6) _____ other (7) _____ for students from class three to eight. For more (8) _____ please (9) _____ any badge (10) _____ of Environment Club.

(11) _____

(12) _____

1.	a) Notice	b) heading	c) date	d) signature
2.	a) Notice	b) heading	c) date	d) content
3.	a) content	b) date	c) Notice	d) heading
4.	a) created	b) made	c) organised	d) brought
5.	a) issue	b) topic	c) medium	d) nature
6.	a) few	b) little	c) more	d) many
7.	a) events	b) things	c) activities	d) rally
8.	a) ideas	b) knowledge	c) know	d) information
9.	a) ask	b) speak	c) tell	d) contact
10.	a) carrier	b) receiver	c) holder	d) worker
11.	a) Notice	b) date	c) heading	d) name
12.	a) heading	b) date	c) post	d) signature

EXERCISE 2

Read the telephonic conversation and fill in the blanks to complete the message.

Mrs Priyanka: Hello!
Nishant: Hello! May I know who is calling?
Mrs Priyanka: I am Priyanka. May I speak to Sushmita?
Nishant: I am sorry. She has just gone out. I am Nishant, her son. Would you like to leave a message?

Mrs Priyanka: Yes, kindly tell her that tomorrow, the Women's Division of the club is organising a get-together in the evening. She should reach the club by 7 pm.

Nishant: Sure, I will convey your message to mom as soon as she comes back. Anything else?
Mrs Priyanka: Oh, yes. Tell her to relay the same message to Mrs Saxena.
Nishant: Sure.

Mrs Priyanka: Thank you very much.
Nishant: You are welcome.

Message

(1) _____

                                              (2) _____

Dear (3) _____,

Your friend, Mrs Priyanka (4) _____ to (5) _____ that you have to (6) _____ the club by 7 pm (7) _____. A get-together (8) _____ by the Women's Division of the club. She has also (9) _____ you to relay this (10) _____ to Mrs Saxena as (11) _____.

(12) _____

1.	a) date	b) time	c) place	d) year
2.	a) day	b) time	c) date	d) year
3.	a) Priyanka	b) Nishant	c) Mom	d) None
4.	a) called up	b) said	c) spoke	d) told
5.	a) say	b) speak	c) tell	d) inform
6.	a) arrive	b) come	c) land	d) reach
7.	a) today	b) tonight	c) day after	d) tomorrow
8.	a) is organised	b) will be organised	c) had been organised	d) has been organised
9.	a) told	b) said	c) ordered	d) requested
10.	a) information	b) conversation	c) idea	d) message
11.	a) soon	b) and	c) old	d) well
12.	a) Mom	b) Mrs Priyanka	c) Nishant	d) Sushmita

EXERCISE 3

Complete Anil's diary entry expressing his feelings a day before the exam.

(1) _____

(2) _____

Dear diary,

My (3) _____ start tomorrow and I am feeling quite (4) _____. Tomorrow is my first exam. Yes, things are not as (5) _____ as I (6) _____ them to be. Until my Math's paper is (7) _____, I won't be able to (8) _____ talk properly. I have (9) _____ had a very sound sleep and now I'm (10) _____ it so much! Every night, I wake up (11) _____ any reason at all. And to add to the problems, just when I try to study, my eyes start (12) _____. But, I am sure I can challenge the (13) _____ and do pretty (14) _____ in my paper in the (15) _____ and come home victorious.

(16) _____

1.	a) date	b) to diary	c) to me	d) today
2.	a) date	b) day	c) today	d) to me
3.	a) examinations	b) day	c) morning	d) tomorrow
4.	a) happy	b) scared	c) nice	d) good
5.	a) difficult	b) calm	c) big	d) easy
6.	a) want	b) show	c) feel	d) expected
7.	a) gone	b) done	c) finished	d) over
8.	a) but	b) even	c) if	d) so
9.	a) never	b) once	c) before	d) always
10.	a) loving	b) enjoying	c) missing	d) leaving
11.	a) for	b) because	c) without	d) no
12.	a) opening	b) moving	c) sleeping	d) closing
13.	a) thing	b) paper	c) school	d) situation
14.	a) as	b) bad	c) well	d) normal
15.	a) tomorrow	b) night	c) morning	d) never
16.	a) Anil	b) date	c) diary	d) yours

COMPREHENSION

EXERCISE 1

Read the passage given below and answer the questions.

Rainbows are often seen when the Sun comes out after or during rain. Rainbows are caused when sunlight shines through drops of water in the sky at a specific angle. When white sunlight enters a raindrop, it exits the raindrop turning a different colour. When light exits lots of different raindrops at different angles, it produces the red, orange, yellow, green, blue, indigo, and violet colours that you see in a rainbow. Together, these colours are known as the spectrum. These colours can sometimes be seen in waterfalls and fountains as well. Did you know that there are double rainbows? In a double rainbow, light reflects twice inside water droplets and forms two arcs. In most double rainbows, the colour of the top arc are opposite to those in the bottom arc. In other words, the order of colours starts with purple on top and ends with red at the bottom. Believe it or not, rainbows sometimes appear as white arcs at night. These rainbows are called moonbows. Moonbows are caused by moonlight (rather than sunlight) shining through drops of water.

1. **Rainbows are often seen**

   a) after rain
   b) before rain
   c) after the sun sets at night
   d) before a storm

2. **Rainbows occur when _____.**

   a) light exits many raindrops at different angles
   b) the sun causes a rainstorm
   c) the spectrum causes a rainstorm
   d) the sun comes out after a storm

3. **Which colour is NOT in a rainbow?**

   a) Yellow
   b) Indigo
   c) Orange
   d) Pink

4. **Which of the following IS NOT true?**

   a) Double rainbows are two rainbows that are exactly the same.
   b) Spectrum colours sometimes appear in fountains and waterfalls.
   c) Moonbows are caused by moonlight.
   d) Rainbows are usually seen after or during rain.

5. **What would be a good title for this passage?**
   a) The History of Rainbows
   b) Differences between Normal Rainbows and Double Rainbows
   c) Moonbows!
   d) The Basics about Rainbow

6. **What colour is a moonbow?**
   a) White
   b) Yellow
   c) Green
   d) The passage doesn't say

Fill in the blanks.

7. **These colours can sometimes be seen in _____ and fountains as well.**
   a) hills
   b) oceans
   c) mountains
   d) waterfalls

8. **When white sunlight enters a _____, it splits into different colours.**
   a) rainbow
   b) tunnel
   c) raindrop
   d) lake

9. **In a double rainbow, light _____ twice inside water droplets and forms two arcs.**
   a) projects
   b) emits
   c) reflects
   d) disappears

10. **Together, these colours are known as the _____.**
    a) rainbow
    b) light
    c) moonbow
    d) spectrum

EXERCISE 2

The Amazon is the world's largest tropical rainforest. It covers an area of nearly 2.8 million square miles, which is nearly the size of Australia. The Amazon Rainforest gets its life from the Amazon River, the world's second largest river, which runs directly through the heart of the region. The rainforest itself is simply the drainage basin for the river and its many tributaries. The vast forest itself consists of four layers, each featuring its own ecosystems and specially adapted plants and animals. The forest floor is the lowest region. Since only two per cent of the sunlight filters through the top layers to the understory, very few plants grow here. The forest floor, however, is rich with rotting vegetation and the bodies of dead organisms, which are quickly broken down into nutrients integrated into the soil. Tree roots stay close to these available nutrients and decomposers, such as millipedes and earthworms, use these nutrients for food. The understory is the layer above the forest floor. Much like the forest floor, only about two to five per cent of the sunlight reaches this shadowy realm. Many of the plants in the understory have large, broad leaves to collect as much sunlight as possible. The understory is so thick that there is very little air movement. As a result, plants rely on insects and animals to pollinate their flowers. The layer above the understory is the canopy. This is where much of the action in the rainforest occurs. Many canopy leaves have specially adapted leaves which form "drip tips". Drip tips allow water to flow off the leaves which prevents mosses, fungi, and lichens from occupying the leaves. Leaves in the canopy are very dense and filter about 80 per cent of the sunlight. The canopy is where the wealth of the rainforest's fruits and flowers grow. Bromeliads, cup-like plants, provide drinking pools for animals and breeding locations for tree frogs. The emergent layer is above the canopy, and is the top layer of the rainforest. Trees in the emergent layer break through the canopy and may reach heights of 200 feet. Leaves in the emergent layer are small and covered with a special wax to hold water. Seeds are blown to other parts of the forest. Trees which rise to the emergent layer are massive. Many are braced by huge buttress roots. Trunks can be 16 feet in circumference. Many animals that survive in the emergent layer never touch the ground.

1. **The Amazon Rainforest covers an area nearly the size of the continent of _____.**
   a) China b) India c) Britain d) Australia

2. **Which of the following is not a layer of the rainforest?**
   a) Understory b) Canopy c) Subcanopy d) Emergent

3. **Which layer of the rainforest is right above the forest floor?**
   a) Canopy b) Emergent Layer c) Understory d) Forest Floor

4. **Most of the fruits and flowers of the rainforest grow in its _____.**
   a) Understory b) Emergent Layer c) Forest Floor d) Canopy

5. **_____ provide drinking pools for animals and breeding locations for tree frogs.**
   a) Petunia b) Bottlebrush c) Pitcher d) Bromeliads

6. **Many trees in the _____ of the rainforest are braced by huge buttress roots.**
   a) Canopy b) Emergent Layer c) Forest Floor d) Understory

7. **Animals that live in the _____ may never touch the ground.**
   a) Emergent Layer b) Canopy c) Forest Floor d) Understory

8. **Why do few plants grow in the understory?**
   a) Their leaves are too large.
   b) There is not enough water.
   c) There is not enough sunlight.
   d) There are not enough nutrients.

9. **Why do plants in the understory have to rely on insects to pollinate them?**
   a) There is very little wind in the understory.
   b) There are very few butterflies in the rainforest.
   c) The sun is too bright in the understory.
   d) The wind is too strong and seeds blow into the Amazon River.

10. **Which of the following is NOT true?**
    a) The Amazon Rainforest is located in South America.
    b) The Canopy is higher than the Emergent Layer.
    c) Leaves in the canopy are very dense and filter a high percentage of sunlight.
    d) The Understory is below the Canopy.

EXERCISE 3

You never saw such a (1) _____ up and down a house, in all your life, as when my Uncle Podger (2) _____ to do a job. A picture would have come home from the frame-maker's, and be standing in the dining-room, (3) _____ to be put up; and Aunt Podger would ask what was to be done with it, and Uncle Podger would say, "Oh, you leave that to me. Don't you, any of you, (4) _____ yourselves about that. I'll do all that."

And then he would take (5) _____ his coat, and begin. He would send the girl out for six penny worth of nails, and then one of the boys after her to tell her what size to get; and, from that, he would (6) _____ work down, and start the whole house.

"Now you go and get me my (7) _____, Will," he would shout; "and you bring me the rule, Tom; and I shall want the (8) step- _____, and I had better have a kitchen-chair, too; and, Jim! You run round to Mr. Goggles, and tell him, 'Pa's kind regards, and hopes his leg's better; and will he lend him his (9) _____ -level?' And don't you go, Maria, because I shall want somebody to hold me the light; and when the girl comes back, she must go out again for a bit of (10) _____ -cord; and Tom!—where's Tom? Tom, you come here; I shall want you to hand me up the picture."

And then he would lift up the picture, and (11) _____ it, and it would come out of the (12) _____, and he would try to save the glass, and cut himself; and then he would (13) _____ round the room, looking for his (14) _____. He could not find his handkerchief, because it was in the pocket of the coat he had taken off, and he did not know where he had put the coat, and all the house had to leave off looking for his (15) _____, and start looking for his coat; while he would dance round and (16) _____ them.

1. a) emotion   b) motion   c) commotion   d) anxiety
2. a) gave   b) undertook   c) left   d) destroyed
3. a) walking   b) shouting   c) sleeping   d) waiting
4. a) enjoy   b) laugh   c) smile   d) worry
5. a) on   b) out   c) in   d) off
6. a) thoroughly   b) gradually   c) stupidly   d) quickly
7. a) nut   b) hammer   c) bolt   d) sickle
8. a) stair   b) mom   c) ladder   d) stick
9. a) heart   b) body   c) spirit   d) mind
10. a) image   b) photo   c) card   d) picture
11. a) fall   b) throw   c) drop   d) push
12. a) box   b) frame   c) panel   d) glass
13. a) crawl   b) laugh   c) speak   d) spring
14. a) paper   b) shirt   c) bow   d) handkerchief
15. a) equipment   b) materials   c) things   d) tools
16. a) allow   b) push   c) insult   d) hinder

EXERCISE 4

Beware of the monsters
Who dwell in the mind,
Who grow in the shelter
Of shadows they find.

Beware of the demons
Who hide from the light,
Who only survive
When our spirits lose sight.

Those creatures can thrive
Where our knowledge is low;
They fill in the spaces
Of what we don't know.

Beware of the monsters
That cause us to hate,
To strike out in anger
When we can't relate.

For ignorance darkens
The mind and the heart,
And helps all our monsters
To tear us apart.

But learning and thinking
Will strengthen us so
We won't be the places
Where monsters can grow.

1. **Where can monsters grow?**

   a) on other planets
   b) in dark ocean caves
   c) in the movies
   d) in our minds

2. **What helps these monsters grow?**

   a) plant food
   b) evil magic
   c) ignorance
   d) anger

3. **What can prevent the monsters from growing?**

   a) learning about others
   b) bravery
   c) weapons
   d) hating those who are different

4. **The author compares ignorance to darkness, and _____ to light.**

   a) the suns
   b) laughter
   c) morals
   d) knowledge

Spoken and written expression

12

EXERCISE 1

Choose the best answers.

1. **Rohit: It was a pleasure to have you. Thanks for coming.**

   Anand: _____.
   a) It's ok.
   b) No problem.
   c) Thank you. The pleasure is all mine.
   d) None of the above.

2. **You are paying for your food at a restaurant. Your bill is 400 and you give the waiter a 500 rupees note. You will say _____.**

   a) This is 500. Please keep the change.
   b) It's so expensive.
   c) Give me some discount.
   d) Take it and leave.

3. **You recently visited Mumbai and you are sharing your experience with your friend.**

   a) I got bored.
   b) It's a very crowded city.
   c) There are film stars everywhere.
   d) Oh! I had an amazing time! It's a very vibrant place.

4. **Sandeep: Excuse me, I think I have lost my way. Can you tell me which way I should go to reach the metro station?**

   Rakesh: Sure, please come along.
   Sandeep: _____.
   a) Thank God I met you.
   b) That's lucky of me.
   c) Will you?
   d) Thanks a lot. That's very kind of you.

5. **You have reserved a table in the name of Vipin at a restaurant. On reaching there, you will say _____.**

   a) You reserved a table in the name of Vipin.
   b) Show me my table.

51

    c) Hello. My name is Vipin. I have a reservation.
    d) None of the above

6. **Akshay: What are you mad about?**

    Piyush: About what happened yesterday.
    Akshay: Can I be of any help?
    Piyush: _____
    a) What will you do?
    b) I can handle myself.
    c) It's not your business.
    d) Thank you for your concern.

7. **Soham: Oh no! I have lost my notebook!**

    Tanmay: _____
    a) How? Where did you leave it?
    b) How forgetful you are!
    c) I pity you.
    d) None of the above

8. **Ankit: Can you pick me up from the mall in the evening?**

    Tarun: _____
    a) Will see.
    b) Why should I?
    c) You come on your own.
    d) Sure, I will be there.

9. **Anuj: Can you pass me some salt please?**

    Ankur: _____
    a) Take it yourself.
    b) Sure, just a moment.
    c) Why do you want it?
    d) None of the above

10. **Teacher: Congratulations, you have done well.**

    Mudit: _____
    a) I know.
    b) I had to.
    c) It's ok.
    d) Thank you very much.

MODEL TEST PAPER-I

Read the questions carefully and answer.

1. A baby learns the meaning of words as _____ are spoken by others and later uses _____ in sentences.

    a) their, they
    b) they, them
    c) they, themselves
    d) it, them

2. Some of these books are _____, and the rest of _____ belong to Shishir.

    a) my, them
    b) hers, their
    c) me, they
    d) mine, them

3. As for _____, I prefer to let people make up _____ minds.

    a) myself, each other's
    b) I, his own
    c) mine, one another's
    d) me, their own

4. I always have my hair cut at Johnson's, as _____ cuts it as well as he does.

    a) anyone
    b) someone else's
    c) no one else
    d) everyone

5. They decided to buy the house because _____ location would allow _____ to travel to work very easily.

    a) theirs, them
    b) it, themselves
    c) its, them
    d) they, us

Tick the synonyms.

6. **Acknowledge**

    a) accept
    b) notice
    c) recognise
    d) start

7. **Bargain**

    a) contract
    b) negotiate
    c) agreement
    d) affirm

8. **Bleak**

    a) barren
    b) discouraging
    c) boring
    d) depressing

9. **Elaborate**

a) complex b) ornate
c) detailed d) original

Tick the antonyms.

10. **Agony**

a) anger b) brutality
c) sensitive d) comfort

11. **Demote**

a) truth b) rectify
c) promote d) secure

12. **Demented**

a) realise b) rational
c) spirited d) demean

13. **Guilty**

a) innocent b) greedy
c) wanted d) hungry

Choose the correct synonym.

14. **Peril**

a) happiness b) action
c) safety d) danger

15. **Forsake**

a) abandon b) sustain
c) chastise d) grace

16. **Wicked**

a) wrong b) evil
c) contagious d) helpful

17. **Credulous**

a) shrewd b) difficult
c) cautious d) gullible

Choose the correct antonym.

18. **Affirmative**
    a) great
    b) hopeful
    c) positive
    d) negative

19. **Elementary**
    a) new
    b) specific
    c) advanced
    d) start

20. **Debar**
    a) stop
    b) push
    c) debris
    d) allow

21. **Spurious**
    a) negative
    b) replica
    c) authentic
    d) difficult

Fill in the blanks.

22. My father would know what to do, only if he _____ here.
    a) was been
    b) has been
    c) were
    d) none of the above

23. If she _____ her notes earlier, she would have passed.
    a) would have gone over
    b) had gone over
    c) has gone over
    d) none of the above

24. Hardly had he moved a little further, the firecracker _____ .
    a) move off
    b) gave up
    c) came off
    d) went off

25. He was caught by his brother as soon as he _____ of the theatre.
    a) got up
    b) got out
    c) moved away
    d) went off

26. A driver _____ follow the rules.
    a) must
    b) should
    c) may
    d) could

27. The sick man has nobody to _____ him.
    a) see off
    b) go off
    c) put off
    d) look after

28. The machine turns off _____.
   a) relatively
   b) fast
   c) magically
   d) automatically

29. They listened _____ to the instructions.
   a) attentively
   b) consciously
   c) clearly
   d) openly

30. They walked _____ along the beach.
   a) seriously
   b) slowly
   c) patiently
   d) noisily

31. They lived as _____ as possible because of their father's unemployment.
   a) poorly
   b) cheaply
   c) casually
   d) miserly

32. They cheered _____ for their team, urging them to push on.
   a) enthusiastically
   b) gladly
   c) angrily
   d) nobly

33. The owner assured that by the end of this year, this tree _____ fruit.
   a) would bear
   b) is going to bear
   c) will be bear
   d) is bearing

34. Several coconut trees _____ by lightning.
   a) have been struck
   b) were struck
   c) is struck
   d) had struck

35. _____ you practice hard, you can't win the quiz.
   a) Until
   b) Unless
   c) Till
   d) If

36. In _____ countries, people drive by the right.
   a) a lot of
   b) whole
   c) many
   d) little

37. Only _____ students went on the trip.
   a) a little
   b) a few
   c) much
   d) more

38. This isn't real, _____?
   a) is it
   b) isn't it
   c) wasn't it
   d) was it

39. Maria has always been your favourite, _____?

    a) has she   b) hasn't she
    c) wasn't she   d) was she

40. This does not mean that we are out of the race, _____ it?

    a) didn't   b) does
    c) did   d) don't

Model Test Paper-2

Choose the correct synonym.

1. **Sterile**
   a) fertile
   b) barren
   c) useless
   d) numb

2. **Prohibit**
   a) access
   b) pave
   c) forbid
   d) enhance

3. **Vivid**
   a) timid
   b) instructive
   c) graphic
   d) obscure

Choose the correct antonym.

4. **Opponent**
   a) rival
   b) foe
   c) confidant
   d) enemy

5. **Young**
   a) ripe
   b) aged
   c) fresh
   d) emerge

6. **Myth**
   a) fact
   b) tale
   c) fiction
   d) vision

Choose the correct spelling.

7. a) museum
   b) musium
   c) mussuem
   d) musiam

8. a) serees
   b) series
   c) ceries
   d) seerees

9. a) tuition
   b) tution
   c) tusion
   d) tushion

10. a) perticular b) partiecular
     c) particular d) partculer

Choose the correct meaning.

11. **In seventh heaven**
    a) very sad b) very dreamy
    c) fortunate d) extremely happy

12. **Apple of his eye**
    a) loving child b) god loving
    c) fruit loving d) favourite person

13. **Brittle**
    a) understood b) very weak
    c) hard but easily broken d) volatile

14. **Amass**
    a) throw b) heavy
    c) huge d) gather

Fill in the blanks.

15. He _____ not do that; it is against the regulations.
    a) shall b) need
    c) could d) must

16. How _____ he speak to you like that?
    a) will b) shall
    c) can d) dare

17. He _____ want to join the trip if he knew about it.
    a) may b) will
    c) might d) could

18. If you are not careful, you _____ yourself.
    a) hurt b) will hurt
    c) is hurting d) hurts

19. I _____ for you to have dinner with the film star.
    a) have arranged b) arranging
    c) arrange d) have arranged

20. I can work faster when there _____ no one to distract me.

a) were
b) is
c) am
d) are

21. Uncle Mahesh has two nephews but no _____.

a) men
b) brides
c) nieces
d) brides

22. The _____ at the church listened attentively to the preacher.

a) congregation
b) gang
c) spectators
d) bevy

23. The _____ was locked up in a cell.

a) fool
b) bankrupt
c) cripple
d) criminal

24. The entire event was handled by _____.

a) referees
b) players
c) musicians
d) volunteers

25. While in Africa, he got a chance to meet a _____ of natives.

a) group
b) staff
c) party
d) tribe

26. The girl of _____ you spoke won a prize.

a) which
b) what
c) whose
d) whom

27. Is that _____ you had a few days off?

a) what
b) when
c) why
d) where

28. Carol said the work would be done by October, _____ personally I doubt very much.

a) it
b) that
c) when
d) which

29. Find out from _____ when she'll be back.

a) she
b) her
c) hers
d) herself

30. If you can't find your book, you can borrow _____.

a) my
b) me
c) mine
d) myself

31. The hairdresser cuts hair very _____ and skilfully.
    a) famously
    b) quickly
    c) freely
    d) instantly

32. You should practice _____ than before if you wish to be a good boxer.
    a) harder
    b) hardest
    c) as harder as
    d) hard

33. The gazelle was _____ by the lioness.
    a) attacked
    b) attacks
    c) will attack
    d) is attacking

34. He just stared _____ at everyone else.
    a) stupidly
    b) clumsily
    c) cleverly
    d) slowly

35. Is there a doctor on the plane? This guy _____ a heart attack!
    a) has
    b) have
    c) had
    d) is having

36. Put your money where your _____ is.
    a) bank
    b) mouth
    c) house
    d) trust

37. When the mouse laughs at the cat, there is _____ nearby.
    a) a dog
    b) cheese
    c) a hole
    d) danger

38. Busy as a _____.
    a) baker
    b) banker
    c) bee
    d) bear

39. Out of sight, out of _____.
    a) trouble
    b) crime
    c) mind
    d) time

40. _____ and steady wins the race.
    a) Slow
    b) Lazy
    c) Ready
    d) Quick

MODEL TEST PAPER-3

Choose the correct answers and fill in the blanks.

1. My fingers were injured so my sister had to write the note _____ me.
   a) by b) for
   c) with d) to

2. What is so good _____ this new movie?
   a) of b) on
   c) for d) about

3. My best friend, John, is named _____ his great-grandfather.
   a) after b) to
   c) about d) on

4. I told Mom we'd be home _____ an hour or so.
   a) to b) in
   c) at d) of

Change the following into indirect speech.

5. Santosh said to the judge, "I did not commit this crime."
   a) Santosh told to the judge that he did not committed the crime.
   b) Santosh told the judge that he had not committed that crime.
   c) Santosh told the judge that he had not committed the crime.
   d) Santosh told to the judge that he had not committed this crime.

6. He said to me, "Where have you lost the pen I brought for you yesterday?"
   a) He asked me where I had lost the pen he had brought for me the day before.
   b) He asked me where I had lost the pen he had brought for me the next day.
   c) He asked me where I had lost the pen he brought for me the previous day.
   d) He asked me where I had lost the pen he had brought for me the previous day.

7. Nandini wrote in her report, "The rainfall has been less till now."
   a) Nandini reported that the rainfall has been less till then.
   b) Nandini reported that the rainfall had been less till now.
   c) Nandini reported that the rainfall has been less till now.
   d) Nandini reported that the rainfall had been less till then.

Change the following to direct speech.

8. **I warned her that I could no longer tolerate her coming late.**

   a) I said to her, "He can no longer tolerate her coming late."
   b) I said to her, "I can no longer tolerate your coming late."
   c) I said to her, "You can no longer tolerate my coming late."
   d) I said to her, "I can no longer tolerate she coming late."

9. **The mother exclaimed that it was clever of him to have solved the puzzle so quickly.**

   a) "How clever you have to be to solve the puzzle so quickly?" said the mother.
   b) "How clever of you to solve the puzzle so fast!" said the mother.
   c) "How clever of you to have solved the puzzle so quickly!" said the mother.
   d) The mother expressed that he was so clever to have solved the quickly.

Choose the correct answer.

10. **When it is time, the prey becomes the _____.**

    a) hungry   b) wary
    c) hunter   d) dinner

11. **What does "rack one's brains" mean?**

    a) let the brain have a rest
    b) damage one's brain
    c) can't think out solutions to the problem
    d) think very hard or for a long time

12. **Once in a blue _____.**

    a) lagoon   b) balloon
    c) moon   d) shoe

13. **Jack of all trades is master of _____.**

    a) some   b) few
    c) fun   d) none

14. **You would give up your seat for a pregnant woman on the bus, _____ you?**

    a) will   b) won't
    c) would   d) wouldn't

15. **I don't have anything on my teeth, _____ I?**

    a) don't   b) didn't
    c) do   d) does

16. He was _____ the best math teacher the school could find.
    a) undoubtedly b) increasingly
    c) tremendously d) minutely

17. I need a contract that has to be _____ possible to cover all grounds.
    a) specific b) more specific
    c) most specific d) as specific as

18. The headmistress promised _____ a long break after a stressful semester.
    a) herself b) ourselves
    c) yourselves d) yourself

19. Jerry _____ the tree to get his kite that is stuck there.
    a) climbed b) has climbed
    c) is climbing d) climb

20. The cough syrup _____ in June and Rahul was about to have it.
    a) will expire b) had expired
    c) expires d) is expiring

21. A fountain _____ built in the centre of the courtyard by the end of the month.
    a) will be b) been
    c) be d) being

22. This kind of robbery has _____ happened in the city before.
    a) often b) many
    c) always d) never

23. Mr Dayal tells the _____ jokes in town.
    a) as funny as b) funny
    c) funniest d) funnier

24. Can you do the job _____? I'm afraid not.
    a) all by yourself b) for yourself
    c) by you d) of yourself

25. It'll be a long time _____ we have another trip.
    a) that b) until
    c) since d) before

26. Will it be possible to make _____ a little earlier?
    a) you b) yourself
    c) this d) it

27. I would love to join the party but I've already got _____ that evening.
    a) anything in
    b) something in
    c) something on
    d) anything on

28. These are the last two marshmallows left in the shop. You can have _____ of them.
    a) one
    b) both
    c) neither
    d) any

29. I prefer making toys for my children _____ them from the shops.
    a) rather than buying
    b) rather buy
    c) rather than to buy
    d) rather buying

30. It isn't getting any better. You had better _____ a doctor.
    a) consult to
    b) consult
    c) consult by
    d) consult with

31. Books should not be left near the open fire. They might _____ easily.
    a) catch fire
    b) catch with fire
    c) catch to fire
    d) catch on fire

32. When will the meeting _____?
    a) be held
    b) be hold
    c) hold place
    d) take hold

33. Would you like to _____ this weekend?
    a) go ski
    b) go skiing
    c) go to ski
    d) skiing

34. I have had _____ for today. I am going home.
    a) enough office
    b) enough of office
    c) office enough
    d) enough office of

35. I _____ yesterday.
    a) went for a walk
    b) had been going for a walk
    c) went for walk
    d) go for a walk

36. He got angry before I _____ a word.
    a) have said
    b) had said
    c) said
    d) has said

37. If I _____ this I shall be wrong.
    a) do
    b) did
    c) done
    d) will do

65

38. He said that he _____ him the day before.
   a) saw b) had seen
   c) was seeing d) seen

39. Rita asked _____ she could go home.
   a) weather b) whom
   c) where d) whether

40. When I _____ to Mumbai I will see him.
   a) will go b) went
   c) go d) may go

Model Test Paper-4

Choose the correct synonym.

1. **germinate**
   a) grow
   b) unnecessary
   c) lethal
   d) impossible

2. **anticipate**
   a) quarrel
   b) battle
   c) expect
   d) countless

3. **indispensable**
   a) irrelevant
   b) unwanted
   c) essential
   d) calm

4. **marginal**
   a) important
   b) minimal
   c) significant
   d) stupid

Choose the correct antonym.

5. **tactful**
   a) clumsy
   b) alert
   c) agog
   d) available

6. **splurge**
   a) spent
   b) save
   c) withdraw
   d) offer

7. **unscathed**
   a) damaged
   b) sound
   c) wholesome
   d) intact

8. **browse**
   a) move
   b) scan
   c) rush
   d) scrutinise

Choose the correct answer.

9. He _____ his school project. He _____ hard on it since last term.
   a) just finish, work
   b) has just finished, has been working
   c) has finished, has working
   d) just finish, been working

10. She _____ her problems with her teacher and she _____ to redo the project.
    a) has been discussing, has decided
    b) discuss, decide
    c) decided, discuss
    d) had discussed, is deciding

11. Ruby _____ to the supermarket. Her friends _____ there the whole morning for her.
    a) just go, wait
    b) gone, waiting
    c) has went, waited
    d) has just gone, have been waiting

12. _____ the two of you, who is weaker in Science?
    a) At
    b) In
    c) Among
    d) Between

13. I will make sure that the plumber _____ here in less than an hour.
    a) getting
    b) gets
    c) will get
    d) got

14. My mother asked me, "_____ to the library with Trisha?"
    a) Can you go
    b) May you go
    c) You can go
    d) Shall you go

15. A gift of appreciation _____ to you if you help out at the charity fair.
    a) are given
    b) is giving
    c) will be given
    d) was given

16. Ruskin's father played an important role in his _____ a writer.
    a) being
    b) turning
    c) changing
    d) becoming

17. This country is backward _____ many aspects.
    a) at
    b) in
    c) on
    d) from

18. Do you think we can bank _____ him?
    a) on
    b) in
    c) at
    d) with

19. Emperor Akbar brought _____ many reforms during his rule.
    a) out
    b) about
    c) up
    d) off

20. She eats anything. She can _____ eat raw potatoes.
    a) even
    b) even if
    c) even so
    d) even that

21. I will do it _____ he forbids me.
    a) even if
    b) even though
    c) even so
    d) even

Change the following sentences from active to passive voice.

22. **The ants are biting me.**
    a) I am being bitten by the ants.
    b) I am being bit by the ants.
    c) I am bitten by the ants.
    d) I was being bitten by the ants.

23. **They are bringing in the luggage.**
    a) The luggage are bringing in by them.
    b) The luggage is brought in by them.
    c) The luggage are brought in by them.
    d) The luggage is being brought in by them.

24. **He broke all the equipment.**
    a) All the equipment broke by him.
    b) All the equipment was broken by him.
    c) All the equipment were broken by him.
    d) All the equipment was broke by him.

Fill in the blanks correctly.

25. We _____ by a loud noise during the night.
    a) woke up
    b) are woken up
    c) were woken up
    d) were waking up

26. There is somebody walking behind us. I think _____ .
    a) we are following
    b) we are being followed
    c) we are followed
    d) we are being following

27. Where _____?
    a) were you born
    b) are you born
    c) have you been born
    d) did you born

Choose the correct answer.

28. a) Cucumber slices some tomato and cut.
    b) Slices some tomato and cut cucumber.

        c) Slices some tomato cucumber and cut.
        d) Cut some cucumber and tomato slices.

29. a) He the ball so hit lost it was that hard.
    b) He hit the ball so hard that it was lost.
    c) Lost it was that he the ball so hit hard.
    d) So hit hard lost it was that he the ball.

30. a) It is very kind of you to help me.
    b) Help you of is it to me kind very.
    c) It to me kind very help you of is.
    d) You of is kind very help it to me.

Choose the correct meaning.

31. **spontaneous**

    a) unsolicited
    b) unable to do anything
    c) confused
    d) excited

32. **hallucination**

    a) unable to hear anything
    b) seeing or hearing things that are not really there
    c) unable to see anything
    d) a dream

33. **take one to task**

    a) criticise or scold someone
    b) to disagree with someone
    c) to praise someone
    d) to convince someone

34. **rapt attention**

    a) with less interest
    b) with complete attention
    c) with great joy
    d) with no attention at all

35. **infiltrate**

    a) group of attackers
    b) men from neighbouring country
    c) terrorists
    d) secretly and gradually gain access

Choose the correct answer.

36. There has been _____ discontentment among the workers in the factory.

    a) few
    b) less
    c) many
    d) much

37. The contractors couldn't have left yet, _____ ?

    a) could they
    b) couldn't they
    c) haven't they
    d) shouldn't they

38. This is my favourite restaurant. No other restaurant serves pasta better than _____ does.

a) it
b) us
c) him
d) they

39. There are a number of good restaurants. _____ you choose is fine with me.

a) Which
b) What
c) Whose
d) Whichever

40. He has put _____ his differences with Tanmay.

a) up
b) off
c) only
d) aside

MODEL TEST PAPER-5

Choose the correct answer.

1. This is one of the best movies that _____ this year.
   a) have been released
   b) were released
   c) was released
   d) have released

2. Bribery is one of the charges that _____ against the minister.
   a) have been levelled
   b) is levelled
   c) is being levelled
   d) has been levelled

3. Since December 2015, I _____ him a monthly stipend for fifteen years.
   a) have been giving
   b) should be giving
   c) would be giving
   d) shall be giving

4. Edison _____ newspapers before he became a famous inventor.
   a) was selling
   b) should sell
   c) used to sell
   d) used to have sold

5. Anil _____ two wickets before rain interrupted the match.
   a) had taken
   b) has taken
   c) had took
   d) took

6. The train was late. _____, I managed to arrive on time.
   a) On the contrary
   b) By contrast
   c) Despite that
   d) Incidentally

7. The boy held the box _____ even though his arm hurt _____.
   a) tightly, badly
   b) tight, bad
   c) tightly, bad
   d) tight, badly

8. _____ as fast as she could, she managed to arrive on time.
   a) Being driving
   b) Driven
   c) Having driving
   d) Driving

9. _____ to his workload, the new employee is also given the charge of interns.
   a) For instance
   b) In the same way
   c) Similarly
   d) In addition

10. I have invited Soham. _____ Rajeev is concerned, he doesn't need an invitation.
    a) As far as
    b) As for
    c) While
    a) Whereas

11. She _____ wait for over two years.
    a) was made to
    b) had made to
    c) has made to
    d) would make to

12. It _____ during the music festival last week.
    a) rained
    b) was raining
    c) is raining
    d) has been raining

13. He would have accepted this proposal, if you _____ more courteous.
    a) are
    b) have been
    c) had been
    d) were

14. What I don't understand is why they _____ so long without lodging a complaint?
    a) were to wait
    b) waited
    c) are to wait
    d) were waiting

15. When the storm subsided, we _____ the next village.
    a) continued on to
    b) continued to
    c) continued on
    d) were continued on to

16. I managed to do _____ in the test although I was not feeling _____ at the time.
    a) well, well
    b) good, well
    c) well, good
    d) good, good

17. _____ by rain, the travellers took shelter under a tree.
    a) Driving
    b) Driven
    c) Been driving
    d) Been driven

18. A trimmer is a machine used _____ grass and weeds.
    a) to cut
    b) for cutting
    c) to cutting
    d) none of these

19. To _____ he lost the bet.
    a) noone's surprise
    b) no ones' surprise
    c) no ones surprise
    d) no one's surprise

20. The circus _____ round of applause for the perfectly timed acrobatic stunts.

a) audience received a well deserved
b) audience gave a well deserved
c) audience gave a well deserve
d) audience did receive a well deserved

21. You _____ working hard.

a) definitely been have
b) definitely have been
c) have been definitely
d) have definitely been

22. The thought _____ never entered his head.

a) fail
b) to fail
c) of failing
d) is failed

23. I don't think his books deserve _____.

a) reading
b) to be read
c) read
d) would read

24. A lot of property _____ by the fire.

a) have been destroyed
b) destroyed
c) has been destroyed
d) will be destroyed

25. He _____ guilty of murder.

a) found
b) was found
c) has been found
d) is found

26. This story _____ next month.

a) will be published
b) will publish
c) published
d) would publish

27. The flat _____ when the Bennets were out for dinner.

a) is ransacked
b) has been ransacked
c) was ransacked
d) had ransacked

28. The room _____ and it looks a lot nicer than before.

a) has been refurbished
b) has refurbished
c) refurbished
d) refurbishes

29. _____ a deer leapt out in front of my car.

a) While driving down the road
b) While I was driving down the road
c) I was driving down the road
d) Driving down the road

30. Although it _____ for days, the cricket pitch was in perfect condition.

a) had been raining
b) is raining
c) had raining
d) has been raining

Choose the grammatically correct, meaningful sentences from the given options.

31. a) Was led by the procession politician noted a.
     b) The procession was led by a noted politician.
     c) Led procession politician a by noted the was.
     d) Noted the was led procession politician a by.

32. a) Rain the of in spite reach to time on managed we.
     b) We managed on time in spite to reach the of rain.
     c) We managed to reach on time in spite of the rain.
     d) Of the rain on time in spite to reach we managed.

33. a) We bought some pencils pens erasers and books.
     b) We bought some Pencils Pens Erasers and Books.
     c) We buy some pencils, pens, erasers and books.
     d) We bought some pencils, pens, erasers and books.

34. a) It is as far as I have understood a bad idea.
     b) It is as far as I have understood a bad idea.
     c) It is as far as I have understood, a bad idea.
     d) It is, as far as I have understood, a bad idea.

Read the passage below and answer the questions.

Windsor Palace is the world's largest and oldest continuously inhabited castle. Occupying over 484,000 square feet, it is over 240 times the size of an average house. William the Conqueror, built the first castle between 1070 and 1086, but the castle that exists today was largely built by Edward of Windsor in 1350. Edward of Windsor authorised the construction of a new keep, a large chapel, and new fortifications. From a distance, the castle appears dominated by a massive round tower in its centre. In 1475, King Edward IV authorised construction of St. George's Chapel as a cathedral and royal mausoleum. The chapel became an important destination for pilgrims in the late medieval period and is probably the most famous of the structures within Windsor Palace. During the 1500's and 1600's, Windsor Castle was damaged as a result of various wars. In 1660, however, Charles II became interested in restoring the castle and laid out plans for "The Long Walk," a three-mile long avenue running south from the castle. Charles II also had the royal apartments and St. George's Hall rebuilt. The royal apartments were spectacular, with numerous carvings, frescoes, and tapestries. The artwork acquired during the rebuilding of Windsor Castle became known as the Royal Collection, which remains relatively unchanged today. In 1824, George IV moved into the castle and was granted 3,00,000 pounds to renovate Windsor Castle. The entire castle was remodelled and the architect, Jeffrey Wyattville, succeeded in blending the castle to seem like one entity rather than a collection of buildings. He raised and lowered the heights of various buildings to give them symmetry and improved the appearance and structure of others.

35. Much of Windsor Castle was constructed under the orders of _____.
    a) William the Conqueror
    b) George IV
    c) Edward of Windsor
    d) King Edward IV

36. Which of the following is closest to the definition of "renovate"?
    a) remodel
    b) rebuild
    c) tear down
    d) calculate

37. Who laid out plans for the "Long Walk?"
    a) Charles II
    b) William the Conqueror
    c) Jeffery Wyattville
    d) King Edward IV

38. Who made major renovations to the castle in 1824?
    a) Jeffrey Wyattville
    b) Charles II
    c) George IV
    d) King Edward IV

39. Which of the following was not part of the royal apartments?
    a) tapestries
    b) carvings
    c) stables
    d) frescoes

40. Which statement best describes Windsor Castle?
    a) Larger than a normal house.
    b) Much larger than a normal house.
    c) Somewhat larger than a normal house.
    d) Smaller than a normal house.

Answer Key

Chapter 1
Exercise 1

1. b	2. d	3. c	4. d	5. a
6. c	7. a	8. c	9. b	10. d
11. c	12. a	13. b	14. c	15. a

Exercise 2

1. b	2. d	3. a	4. c	5. d
6. a	7. c	8. b	9. d	10. c
11. c	12. a	13. c		

Exercise 3

1. c	2. d	3. a	4. b	5. b
6. c	7. d			

Chapter 2
Exercise 1

1. a	2. d	3. c	4. d	5. c
6. c	7. d	8. c		

Exercise 2

1. d	2. d	3. a	4. d	5. d

Exercise 3

1. d	2. a	3. b	4. b	5. d
6. b				

Exercise 4

1. d	2. d	3. a	4. c	5. a

Exercise 5

1. d	2. d	3. d	4. d	5. d
6. d	7. d	8. d	9. c	10. c

Exercise 6

1. d	2. c	3. a	4. d	5. b

Chapter 3
Exercise 1

1. c	2. a	3. b	4. c	5. c
6. c	7. b	8. a	9. d	10. b
11. a	12. d	13. a	14. d	15. a

Exercise 2

1. d	2. a	3. a	4. d	5. b
6. a	7. d	8. d	9. b	10. a

Exercise 3

1. c	2. b	3. a	4. d	5. d
6. b	7. b	8. d		

Exercise 4

1. b	2. c	3. d	4. d	5. c
6. d	7. c	8. c	9. d	10. b

Chapter 4

Exercise 1

1. c	2. a	3. c	4. c	5. b
6. a	7. d	8. a	9. c	10. a

Exercise 2

1. b	2. c	3. a	4. d	5. c
6. c	7. b	8. d	9. d	10. d

Exercise 3

1. d	2. a	3. a	4. a	5. a
6. b	7. a	8. a	9. d	10. b
11. b	12. d	13. b	14. a	15. c
16. a	17. b	18. d	19. b	20. a

Chapter 5

Exercise 1

1. a	2. d	3. d	4. c	5. c
6. a	7. a	8. a	9. d	10. a
11. d	12. d	13. a	14. c	15. c

Exercise 2

1. d	2. b	3. c	4. d	5. a

Exercise 3

1. a	2. b	3. d	4. b	5. b
6. d	7. b	8. b	9. a	10. c

Chapter 6

Exercise 1

1. c	2. a	3. c	4. d	5. a
6. c	7. b	8. b	9. a	10. b
11. a	12. c			

Exercise 2

1. d	2. a	3. d	4. d	5. d
6. c	7. c	8. b	9. b	10. c
11. b	12. c	13. b	14. a	

Chapter 7

Exercise 1

1. d	2. d	3. a	4. c	5. b
6. c	7. b	8. d	9. b	10. c

Exercise 2

1. d	2. b	3. b	4. a	5. c
6. a	7. a	8. d	9. c	10. d
11. c	12. a	13. a	14. b	15. c

Chapter 8

1. c	2. b	3. a	4. a	5. a
6. c	7. a	8. c	9. d	10. d
11. b	12. a	13. c	14. d	15. b
16. a	17. c	18. d	19. a	20. a
21. b	22. b	23. a	24. b	
25. b				

Chapter 9

Exercise 1

1. b	2. b	3. d	4. b	5. d
6. d	7. d	8. c		

Exercise 2

1. a	2. c	3. a	4. d	5. d
6. d	7. a	8. d	9. a	10. b
11. c	12. b			

Exercise 3

1. a	2. b	3. d	4. d	5. d
6. a	7. c	8. b	9. d	10. a
11. c	12. c	13. c	14. b	15. d

Chapter 10

Exercise 1

1. a	2. c	3. d	4. c	5. b
6. d	7. c	8. d	9. d	10. c
11. d	12. c			

Exercise 2

1. a	2. a	3. c	4. a	5. d
6. d	7. d	8. d	9. d	10. d
11. d	12. c			

Exercise 3

1. a	2. b	3. a	4. b	5. d
6. d	7. d	8. b	9. d	10. c
11. c	12. d	13. d	14. c	15. c
16. a				

Chapter 11

Exercise 1

1. a	2. a	3. d	4. a	5. d
6. a	7. d	8. c	9. c	10. d

Exercise 2

| 1. d | 2. c | 3. c | 4. d | 5. d |
| 6. b | 7. a | 8. c | 9. a | 10. b |

Exercise 3

1. c	2. b	3. d	4. d	5. d
6. b	7. b	8. c	9. c	10. d
11. c	12. a	13. d	14. d	15. d
16. a				

Exercise 4

| 1. d | 2. c | 3. a | 4. d |

Chapter 12

Exercise 1

| 1. c | 2. a | 3. d | 4. d | 5. c |
| 6. d | 7. a | 8. d | 9. b | 10. d |

Model Test Paper 1

1. b 2. d 3. d 4. c 5. c 6. c 7. b 8. d 9. c 10. d 11. c 12. b 13. a 14. d 15. a 16. b 17. d 18. d 19. c 20. d 21. c 22. c 23. b 24. d 25. b 26. a 27. d 28. d 29. a 30. b 31. b 32. a 33. a 34. a 35. b 36. c 37. b 38. a 39. b 40. b

Model Test Paper 2

1. b 2. c 3. c 4. c 5. b 6. a 7. a 8. b 9. a 10. c 11. d 12. d 13. c 14. d 15. d 16. d 17. c 18. b 19. a 20. b 21. c 22. c 23. d 24. d 25. d 26. d 27. c 28. d 29. b 30. c 31. b 32. a 33. a 34. a 35. d 36. b 37. c 38. c 39. c 40. a

Model Test Paper 3

1. b 2. d 3. a 4. b 5. b 6. c 7. d 8. b 9. c 10. c 11. d 12. c 13. d 14. d 15. c 16. a 17. d 18. a 19. c 20. b 21. a 22. d 23. c 24. a 25. d 26. d 27. c 28. b 29. a 30. b 31. a 32. a 33. b 34. b 35. a 36. b 37. a 38. b 39. d 40. c

Model Test Paper 4

1. a 2. c 3. c 4. b 5. a 6. b 7. a 8. d 9. b 10. a 11. d 12. d 13. b 14. a 15. c 16. d 17. b 18. a 19. b 20. a 21. a 22. a 23. d 24. b 25. c 26. b 27. a 28. d 29. b 30. a 31. a 32. b 33. a 34. d 35. c 36. d 37. a 38. a 39. d 40. d

Model Test Paper 5

1. c 2. d 3. a 4. c 5. a 6. c 7. a 8. d 9. d 10. b 11. a 12. a 13. c 14. b 15. b 16. a 17. b 18. b 19. d 20. b 21. d 22. c 23. b 24. c 25. b 26. a 27. c 28. b 29. b 30. a 31. b 32. c 33. d 34. d 35. c 36. b 37. a 38. c 39. c 40. b